breeze-easy method *1*

by Valentine Anzalone

Cover photo courtesy of the Selmer Company.

FOREWORD

This METHOD offers to the young student a systematic approach to correct concepts in music reading and oboe playing. The method may be used with equally satisfying results either for private study or for class work. The fundamentals of tone production, technique, rhythmic understanding, and tonal consciousness have been especially emphasized. Additionally, this book offers a refreshing repertoire of new song material that will delight both student and teacher.

Through this course of study in which efficiency and thoroughness have been pin-pointed, the student is guided to take his place as a contributing member of the school band or orchestra in the shortest possible time. Upon completion of books I & II of the "BREEZE EASY" METHOD for OBOE, the student will be prepared to enter directly into most intermediate oboe methods.

Valentine C. Anzalone

PLAYING POSITIONS

THE OBOE IN PLAYING POSITION

THE THUMBS IN PLAYING POSITION

THE LIPS AND REED
IN CORRECT PLAYING POSITION

PROPER HAND AND FINGER POSITION

HOW TO READ THE FINGERING GIVEN
IN THIS BOOK

The Oboe has **6** finger holes which are pointed out and represented by the **6** circles in the fingering diagram below.

This sign – ● – tells us that the hole is to be covered.

This sign – ○ – tells us that the hole is kept open.

This sign – ◓ – tells us that only the lower half of the hole is to be covered.

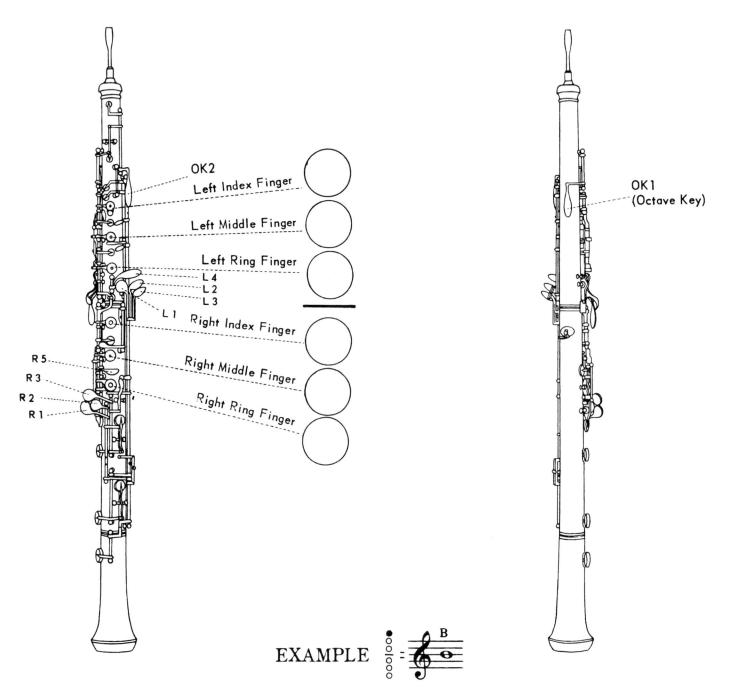

EXAMPLE

The fingering diagram in the example above indicates that you should cover the first finger hole with the left index finger.

(A FINGERING CHART for general reference is given on pages **30** and **31**.)

PRELIMINARY LESSON

THINGS YOU SHOULD KNOW BEFORE WE BEGIN:

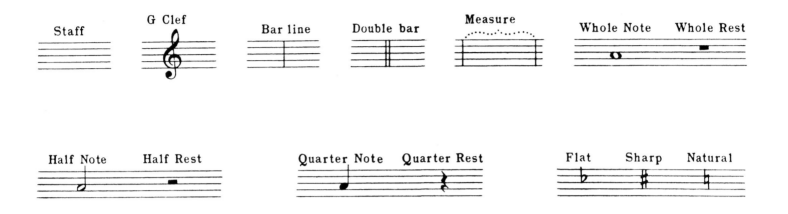

Staff   G Clef   Bar line   Double bar   Measure   Whole Note   Whole Rest

Half Note   Half Rest   Quarter Note   Quarter Rest   Flat   Sharp   Natural

TIME SIGNATURES

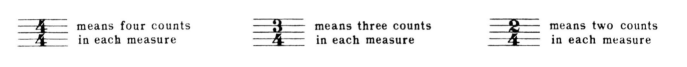

$\frac{4}{4}$ means four counts in each measure $\frac{3}{4}$ means three counts in each measure $\frac{2}{4}$ means two counts in each measure

NAMES OF NOTES

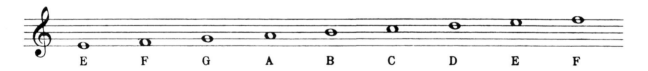

E   F   G   A   B   C   D   E   F

OUR FIRST TONES

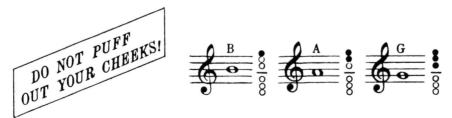

DO NOT PUFF OUT YOUR CHEEKS!

B   A   G

YOUR TEACHER WILL SHOW YOU HOW TO HOLD YOUR INSTRUMENT AND PRODUCE A TONE CORRECTLY. PRACTICE HOLDING EACH OF THE FIRST TONES FOR A LONG WHILE. KEEP TRYING TO IMPROVE YOUR TONE BY LISTENING TO YOURSELF.

(All New Notes and Material will be placed in a box at the beginning of each lesson.)

LESSON 1.

THIS LESSON HAS BEEN COMPLETED.   DATE _____   EXCELLENT ☐ GOOD ☐ FAIR ☐

LESSON 2.

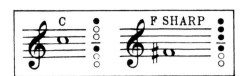

1.

2.

3.

4.

5.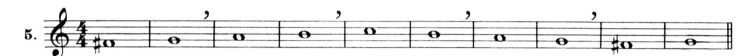

6.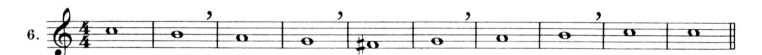

7.

8.

9.

FIRST DUET

10.

THIS LESSON HAS BEEN COMPLETED.   DATE _____   EXCELLENT ☐ GOOD ☐ FAIR ☐

LESSON 3.

♩ = HALF NOTE   ▭ = HALF REST

COUNT: 1 2   3 4   1 2   3 4

COUNT: 1 2   3 4

COUNT: 1 2   3 4   1 2 3 4   1 2

SKIPS

HALF NOTE SONG

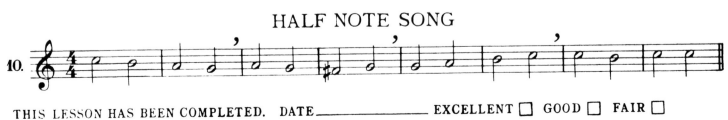

THIS LESSON HAS BEEN COMPLETED.   DATE_____ EXCELLENT ☐ GOOD ☐ FAIR ☐

21566-29

LESSON 4. ♩ = QUARTER NOTE ♩ = QUARTER REST

THE QUARTER REST

A GHOST'S TUNE

V. C. A.

AT PIERROT'S DOOR

THIS LESSON HAS BEEN COMPLETED. DATE_____ EXCELLENT ☐ GOOD ☐ FAIR ☐

21566-29

THE TIE

MARCHING SONG (Duet)

CIRCLE WALTZ

V.C.A.

THIS LESSON HAS BEEN COMPLETED. DATE_____ EXCELLENT ☐ GOOD ☐ FAIR ☐

LESSON 6.

C = COMMON TIME - Same as 4/4

OLD GERMAN SONG

Go quickly to next line

MARY HAD A LITTLE LAMB

REVIEW QUIZ NO. 1

WRITE IN THE NAME OF EACH NOTE GIVEN BELOW

EXAMPLE

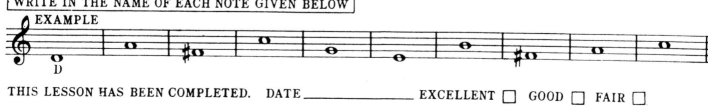

THIS LESSON HAS BEEN COMPLETED.   DATE _____   EXCELLENT ☐   GOOD ☐   FAIR ☐

LESSON 7.

THIS LESSON HAS BEEN COMPLETED. DATE_____ EXCELLENT ☐ GOOD ☐ FAIR ☐

LESSON 8.

KEY OF G
ALL F's ARE SHARP

FIRST AND SECOND ENDINGS

1. Ask your teacher to explain the action of the left index finger in going to and from D.

HALF HOLE PRACTICE

2.

3. THIS MEANS ALL F's ARE SHARP
( ) = JUST A REMINDER

YANKEE DOODLE

4.

5.

FIRST AND SECOND ENDINGS

6. PLAY FIRST TIME ONLY
1.
REPEAT
PLAY SECOND TIME ONLY
2.

A SINGING GAME

7.
1.
2.

THIS LESSON HAS BEEN COMPLETED.   DATE _____   EXCELLENT ☐   GOOD ☐   FAIR ☐

21566-29

LESSON 10.

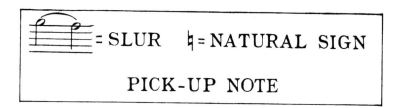

= SLUR ♮ = NATURAL SIGN

PICK-UP NOTE

THE C SCALE (Memorize)

OLD ENGLISH MELODY

ON TOP OF OLD SMOKEY

MARIONETTE'S MARCH (Duet)

THIS LESSON HAS BEEN COMPLETED.   DATE _____ EXCELLENT ☐ GOOD ☐ FAIR ☐

21566-29

LESSON 11.

THE G SCALE (Memorize)

DUKE STREET

B♭ and B♮

ABIDE WITH ME

THIS LESSON HAS BEEN COMPLETED. DATE_____ EXCELLENT ☐ GOOD ☐ FAIR ☐

THE F SCALE (Memorize)

A TISKET, A TASKET

USING "forked F"

Use the x fingering for F ("forked F") whenever F is preceded or followed by a note requiring the use of the right ring finger.

CRUSADER'S HYMN

MARCH OF THE VICTORS

V. C. A

THIS LESSON HAS BEEN COMPLETED. DATE _____ EXCELLENT ☐ GOOD ☐ FAIR ☐

21566-29

LESSON 13.

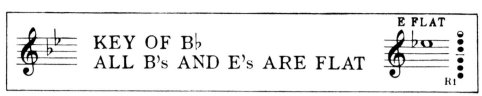

KEY OF B♭
ALL B's AND E's ARE FLAT

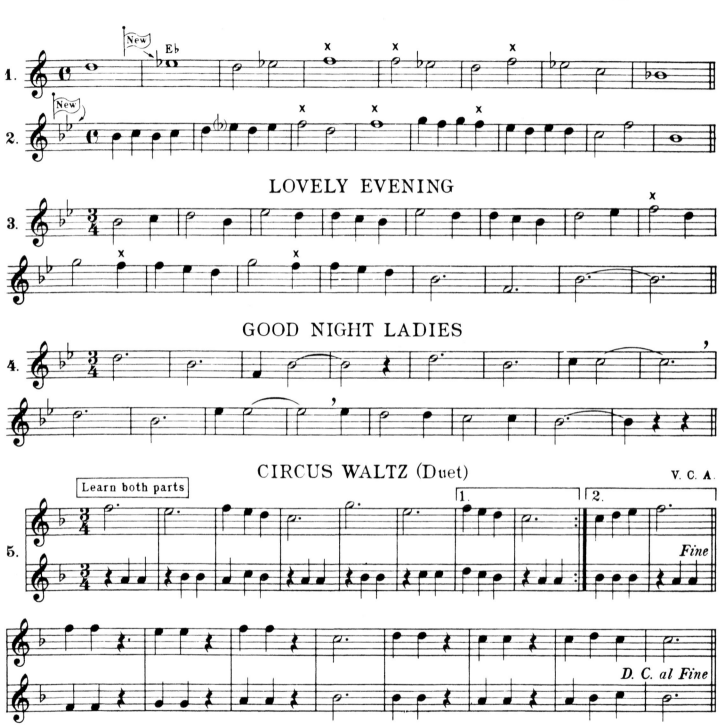

LOVELY EVENING

GOOD NIGHT LADIES

CIRCUS WALTZ (Duet)

V. C. A.

Learn both parts

Fine

D. C. al Fine

REVIEW QUIZ NO. 2

The top number in a time sign tells you how many beats are in a measure, for example, in $\frac{3}{4}$ time there are 3 beats in a measure. Fill in the empty measures given below with note values that will be correct for the time sign given.

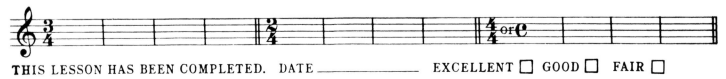

THIS LESSON HAS BEEN COMPLETED. DATE _____ EXCELLENT ☐ GOOD ☐ FAIR ☐

LESSON 14. ♪ ♫ = EIGHTH NOTES ɤ = EIGHTH REST

LESSON 15.

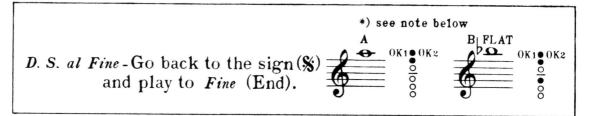

D. S. al Fine - Go back to the sign (𝄋) and play to *Fine* (End).

1.

add OK2 (OK2 is played with the left index finger.)

THE B♭ SCALE (Memorize)

2.

3.

AFTER-BEATS

4.

COUNT: 1 + 2 +

HOW CAN I LEAVE THEE

5.

POODLES ON PARADE

6.

V. C. A.

GO BACK TO THE SIGN (𝄋) AND END AT THE *Fine* WITHOUT REPEAT

* If your Oboe has an Automatic Octave Key, disregard OK2 when it is indicated.

THIS LESSON HAS BEEN COMPLETED. DATE _____ EXCELLENT ☐ GOOD ☐ FAIR ☐

21566 - 29

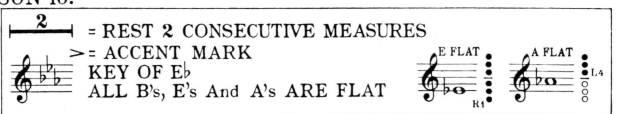

THE LONG REST

THE Eb SCALE (Memorize)

BILLY BOY

Cowboy Song

ACCENT EXERCISE

FANFARE FOR TWO (Duet)

V. C. A.

THIS LESSON HAS BEEN COMPLETED. DATE _____ EXCELLENT ☐ GOOD ☐ FAIR ☐

LESSON 17.

♩ ♩ ♩ ♩ = STACCATO-Detached Notes

G SHARP (same as A♭)

THE STACCATO

1.

MEASURES 1 & 2 SHOULD SOUND ALIKE BECAUSE OF THE STACCATO MARKS IN MEASURE 2

AMARYLLIS

GHYS

2.

CHROMATIC SONG

3.

HAPPY LITTLE DONKEY

Traditional Round

4.

5.

Repeat many times

GOING HOME (Duet)

DVORAK

6.

MELODY BY HAYDN

7.

THIS LESSON HAS BEEN COMPLETED. DATE _____ EXCELLENT ☐ GOOD ☐ FAIR ☐

21566 - 29

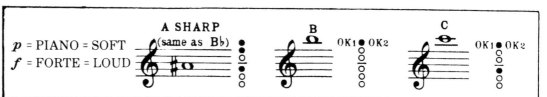

LESSON 19.

♩. = DOTTED QUARTER NOTE

A FLAT

INTRODUCING THE DOTTED QUARTER NOTE

COUNT: 1 + 2 + 3 + 4 +

ALMA MATER

PATRIOTIC HYMN

SLURRING PRACTICE

O COME ALL YE FAITHFUL

THIS LESSON HAS BEEN COMPLETED. DATE _____ EXCELLENT ☐ GOOD ☐ FAIR ☐

21566-29

THE STAR SPANGLED BANNER

THIS LESSON HAS BEEN COMPLETED. DATE _____ EXCELLENT ☐ GOOD ☐ FAIR ☐

26

LESSON 21.

SCALE REVIEW

OH! SUSANNA

BLOW THE MAN DOWN

THE MARINES' HYMN (Duet)

THIS LESSON HAS BEEN COMPLETED. DATE _____ EXCELLENT ☐ GOOD ☐ FAIR ☐

21566 - 29

LESSON 23.

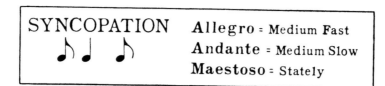

SYNCOPATION

Allegro = Medium Fast
Andante = Medium Slow
Maestoso = Stately

THESE MEASURES ARE PLAYED THE SAME

COUNT: 1 + 2 + 1 2 1 + 2 + 1 2

LIZA JANE

Allegro (Medium Fast)

Traditional

mf staccato

NOBODY KNOWS THE TROUBLE I'VE SEEN

Andante (Medium Slow)

Traditional

mf

A PRAYER

Maestoso (Stately)

CARRY ME BACK TO OLD VIRGINNY

BLAND

mp

Fine

D. S. al Fine

THIS LESSON HAS BEEN COMPLETED. DATE _____ EXCELLENT ☐ GOOD ☐ FAIR ☐

LESSON 24.

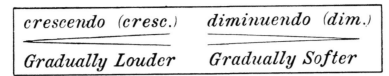

CHROMATIC EXERCISE

CRESCENDO AND DIMINUENDO

PRAISE FOR PEACE

THE CHROMATIC SCALE (Memorize)

SHE'LL BE COMIN' ROUND THE MOUNTAIN

THIS LESSON HAS BEEN COMPLETED. DATE _____ EXCELLENT ☐ GOOD ☐ FAIR ☐

21566-29

*See Notes Below.

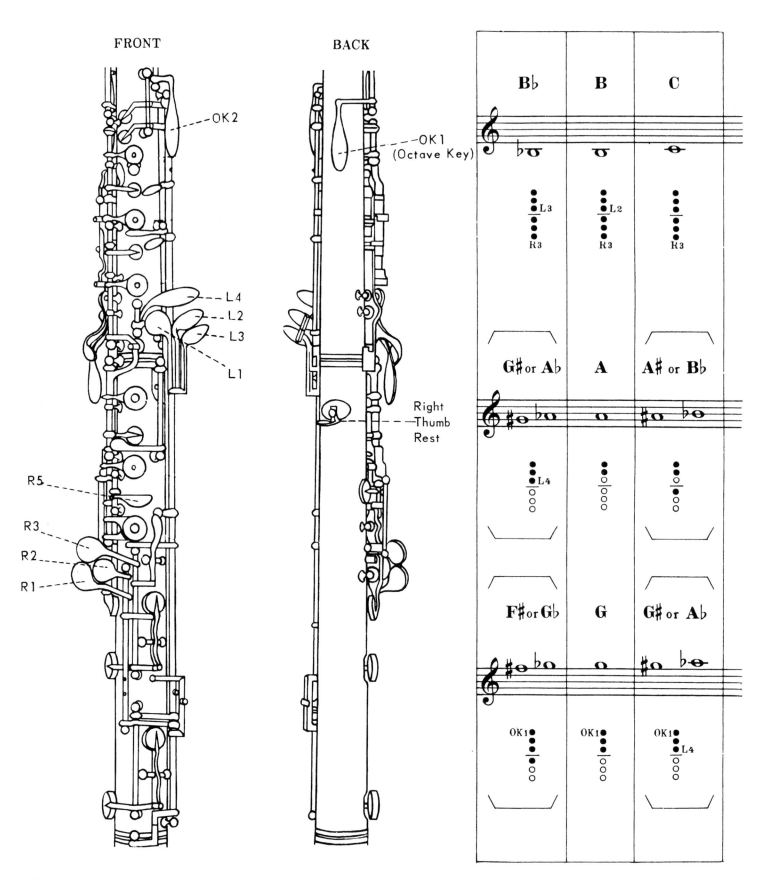

FRONT

BACK

*If your Oboe has key OK1 and key OK2, the use of OK1 is optional from high A to high C.

*If your Oboe has an Automatic Octave Key, disregard OK2 when it is indicated.

*When two notes are given together (G♯ or A♭), they sound alike and therefore are fingered the same.

FINGERING CHART

The pieces on this page may be played as Solos, Duets, Trios and Rounds as indicated under each title. These Ensembles may be played by groups of "like" or "mixed" instruments (Flutes, Oboes, Trumpets, Drums, etc. may play together). When "mixed" groups play these Ensembles, only F Horns and E♭ Saxophones may be used.